DALI/MIRÓ

Dali/Miró

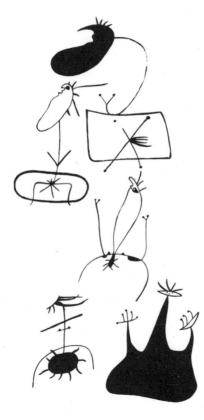

Text and Notes by
PAUL H. WALTON
Chairman, Department of Fine Arts
McMaster University, Canada

TUDOR PUBLISHING COMPANY
New York

Published by

TUDOR PUBLISHING COMPANY

New York, 1967

Library of Congress Catalog Card Number: 67-19837

Miró reproductions permission A.D.A.G.P., 1967,
by French Reproduction Rights, Inc.

Printed in Japan

SALVADOR DALI

The reputation of Salvador Dali has been so aggressively established through self-promotion that it forms a barrier to the calm assessment of his art. People are concerned about whether or not to take seriously the work of a man whose extravagant behavior has for years caught the amused attention of the public at large. Certainly he does not seem to fit the Renaissance conception of the great artist as a man whose dignity, decorum and learning give him an academic status equal to that of poets and philosophers. Instead, Dali strikes many people as a dangerous clown, whose clowning undermines the dignity of art, and whose painting must therefore be dismissed. Yet this is obviously an unfair way to judge a career which can be shown to depend on a principle of deliberate destruction that is meant to be applied to all traditional conceptions of art and artists. In fact, the enunciation of this principle in Dali's work may yet prove to be one of the most important elements in the development of twentieth-century painting.

Dali's early life and education are described in his autobiography, *The Secret Life of Salvador Dali,* with full attention to the fantasies, myths and dreams that he says were so intermingled with his childhood consciousness of the real world, that in looking back he now has difficulty in telling where reality began and the imaginary ended—a point one must keep in mind when attempting to sort out the verifiable facts from the basic myths about his career. He was born in 1904 in the Spanish town of Figueras, the son of a notary, and because an older brother had died at the age of seven, his parents lavished affection on him. For four years, until the birth of a sister, he was a spoiled and only child, cultivating what was to become, by his own ac-

Early years— myth and reality

5

count, a monstrous and brutal egotism. At school he claims
to have played the part of a wealthy and arrogant little aristocrat
in the midst of the ragged children of laborers; and this initiated
a favorite fantasy, in which he became a child king with absolute
powers, thus establishing the basis of his future admiration for
monarchs and dictators.

He was talented and precocious, and began to teach himself
Art
training
painting at least by the age of fourteen, imitating the work of
Spanish Impressionists. When he entered the Madrid School
of Fine Arts in 1921 he distinguished himself by eccentric behavior, great technical skill, and easy familiarity with such avant-
garde tendencies as Cubism, Futurism, and Italian "Metaphysical" painting. However, his constant drive to establish the
uniqueness of his own personality prompted him to attempt a
combination in his work of a realism based on Vermeer and
the Dutch tradition with the fantastic distortions of modern
art. After his expulsion from art school in 1924 for insubordination, he accomplished this by exhibiting meticulously detailed
still lifes, portraits, and landscapes side-by-side with cubist compositions. Unfortunately, both styles imposed unwanted restraints,
the one factual, the other structural, on the free imaginative expression of his genius. A way out was suggested by the metaphysical art of Giorgio de Chirico, in which realistically detailed
Chirico,
Freud
landscapes were given dream-like dislocations of space and
sometimes menacing figures or forms. Further inspiration toward
an art of free fantasy came from reading Freud's *Interpretation
of Dreams* and essay on Leonardo da Vinci, which introduced
Dali to the symbolic imagery by which the subconscious expresses
repressed obsessions and complexes. The result was that in 1927
he began to produce landscape-like paintings in which there
swirled and floated fragmented dream symbols such as skeletons,
birds, parts of human anatomy, and fetish objects. These early
dream fantasies are deliberately loose and accidental in composition, with forms defined by a rhythmic calligraphic touch, so

6

that the pictures suggest spontaneous presentations of the artist's dream world (Plate 4).

In 1928 Dali visited Paris for the first time and became acquainted with the Surrealist writers and painters under the leadership of André Breton. Here he found a movement influenced, like himself, by the new psychology, and devoted to exploring the subconscious psychic environment of human life. He met artists such as Arp, Ernst, Tanguy and Miró, who were evoking the strange and poetic imagery of personal dream worlds by submitting the creative process to the laws of chance in automatic, trance-like outpourings of poetic and pictorial motifs. *Surreal-ism*

With his usual compulsive individuality, Dali, on his return to Spain, developed a distinctive version of Surrealist ideals and methods. Already obsessed with the way Freud had actively interpreted dream images, converting each into a symbol for an intimate aspect of the dreamer's personal life, he now moved beyond this to consider the parallel way in which the insane interpret reality itself, which becomes, for them, a kind of dream. For the paranoid individual, every aspect of reality can be drawn into a logical argument as evidence to support his insane obsessions. Dali conceived of the possibility of an art counterfeiting paranoid delusions, and devoted to the systematic destruction of the real world, rather than to the poetic description of the subconscious that was the preoccupation of other Surrealists. He began to paint works like *The Invisible Man* (Plate 5) of 1929, where fantastic dream shapes are described with meticulous realism, but which, under examination, eventually combine to form a secondary image of a possessed man seated on a pedestal—thus giving pictorial expression to the way the insane may impose double meanings on reality. *Paranoid delu-sions*

"The In-visible Man"

This was the beginning of a brilliant series of paintings in which Dali's technique became more and more realistic, yet at the same time converted the details, colors, textures and forms of the external world into figurations of the obsessions of a mad-

7

man. Bizarre combinations and transformations of forms, combined with multiple, superimposed images, became the theme of an art which Dali produced by what he now described as his "paranoiac-critical" method, "the systematic association of the most delirious phenomena and elements, so as to give tangible creativeness to my most dangerous obsessions."

Why did Dali play the destructive madman, when the other Surrealists were seeking sanity through the integration in art of man's material and psychic environments? Like them, he was motivated by hatred of machinery, technology, and mass movements; but instead of constructing a counter-reality he set out in his art "to cretinize the masses" and "ruin systematically the logical meaning of all the mechanisms of the rational, practical world." Out of the ruins he fashioned new expressions of the old sense of irrational mystery at the heart of things, to which conservative minds, like his own, are attuned—and certainly Dali's opinions and sympathies in favor of traditional institutions like the monarchy, absolutism, and aristocratic privilege leave no doubt as to the radical conservatism of his outlook. This helps to account for the violence of his reaction to the modern threat of democratic and mechanized conformity, and his estrangement from the left-oriented Surrealist group around André Breton.

With equal inevitability Dali's destructive and mystifying art has attracted the patronage of wealthy and socially prominent individuals, and after his first Paris exhibition in 1929 he became the best known of the Surrealists through his flair for publicity, his film-making activities with Luis Bunuel (*Un Chien Andalou,* 1929, and *L'Age d'Or,* 1931), and the publication of books and essays explaining his methods. In 1933 his first New York exhibition took place, followed by a visit to the United States the next year.

After his famous painting of 1931, *The Persistence of Memory,* with its limp watches, his style became increasingly photographic

Reaction against technology

Monarchism

in its realism, until, in 1937, he began to make visits to Italy and the classical style of the Renaissance stimulated a new interest in imposing strict mathematical order on both his realism and his fantasies. This classical ambition, proclaimed in 1941, combined with religious conversion to inspire a continuing series of monumental religious and mythological subjects beginning with *The Madonna of Port Lligat* of 1950 and the famous *Christ of St. John of the Cross* of 1951. The monumental realism of these works, their religious sentiment, and their mystifying references to nuclear physics and Renaissance theories of proportion, as well as the installation of several important examples in large public galleries in New York, Washington and Glasgow, have served to keep Dali's name a focus for continuing controversy and critical attention.

Religion and classicism

JOAN MIRÓ

The art of Joan Miró provides a striking complement and contrast to that of his countryman Dali; for whereas the fantasies and obsessions of the latter seem to have been realized through strenuous efforts of will, imagination and technique, in Miró's work one encounters a spontaneous flow of imagery evolving according to laws of its own. In fact, Dali's art and career show so much calculation and self-awareness that one tends to think of him as a technician and inventor, rather than as an artist who, according to the traditional conception of the poetic process, submits to an inner power greater than himself. Miró is preeminently an artist in this traditional sense, and his career shows a pattern of natural growth and change in his unique vision that can be compared with the kind of development one finds among the greatest ancient and modern masters.

Spontaneous imagery

Miró was born near Barcelona in 1893, and received his art training in that city, first at the Barcelona School of Fine Arts, and then in a private school of applied design. From his earliest teachers he acquired marked technical proficiency, and absorbed the Romanticism of the nineteenth century, particularly its love of landscape and interest in links between the expressive effects of painting, poetry, and music. He made contact with the exciting experiments of young artists in Paris through a meeting with José Dalmau, an art dealer who played an important role in the progressive cultural life of Barcelona by staging exhibitions of works by Fauve and Cubist painters. The startling originality of these new styles could receive sympathetic attention in the city that had already produced Picasso, and where the architect Antoni Gaudi was erecting his fantastic buildings. Thus, it is not so surprising to find that even such early works by Miró as the *Portrait of E. C. Ricart* (Plate 50) and *Landscape Near Montroig* (Plate 49) are radical translations of the familiar features of a friend, in one case, and Miró's native countryside, in the other, into Fauve-inspired patterns of violently flattened and distorted shapes, painted in rainbow hues. Such works were executed before Miró's first visit to Paris in 1919, when he met Picasso, and encountered Cubism at the source. The immediate result of this encounter can be seen in his *Seated Nude* (Plate 52) of 1919, which relinquishes the lively animation of the earlier works in favor of classical calm, sharply incised planes and contours, and cubistic analysis of portions of the figure.

The *Self Portrait* (Plate 47), also from 1919, shows similar features, but in addition it has a "primitive" force, clarity and solemnity that indicates Miró's interest in folk art and the naive art of "Sunday painters" like Picasso's friend, the customs officer Henri Rousseau. This concern had originated in Miró's study of Catalan frescoes from the Middle Ages in the Barcelona National Museum, with their flat, stylized significations of essential forms that take on the aspect of symbols. Picasso's enthusiasm for

Barcelona —early influences

Cubism

Folk Art

similar archaic styles intensified this interest, and led Miró to ignore the tendency in Cubism toward intellectual abstraction, using it instead as a means of giving natural forms an elemental, geometric reality. The resulting combination of cubist geometry and archaic signification is seen best in a series of Spanish landscapes culminating in the large painting of *The Farm* (Plate 54), finished in 1922. This work collects all the essential features of the rural scene in Spain and marks them out with primitive clarity of shape and color within a rigid pattern showing cubist discipline. It is a dignified expression of Miró's concern with recapturing the fresh and wondering awareness of environment that children and folk artists show in fashioning simple signs and symbols for basic elements of their experience.

As a result of this kind of search for archetypal form and meaning Miró was immediately interested when the Surrealists began to suggest ways of probing and defining a subjective realm of primitive realities made up of dreams and unconscious impulses. From them he learned to devote his art to what he called his "hallucinations," with the result that strange apparitions began to flow automatically from his brush. In 1925 he finished *The Harlequin's Carnival* (Plate 56), a room filled with fantastic creatures echoing many of the forms and rhythms of *The Farm,* as though illustrating the way the elements of his external world had become absorbed in the inner landscape of his dreams.

This interior world was found by Miró to be filled with elemental and marvelous images—the stars, sun and moon, snakes and insects, animals and grotesque fragments of human anatomy arranged and combined in ways that evoke primitive feelings of wonder, glee, and terror. As in his Spanish landscapes he wanted to retain a naive sense of wonder in his presentation of these forms, and in a series of "automatic" paintings from about 1925, he tried to get to the very beginnings of the creative process, producing without conscious control vague shapes and simple linear patterns, traced as though by the wavering hand of a

11

child experiencing the first delights of image-making (Plates 58, 59, 60). The result was the use of a more informal and accidental vocabulary of shape, line, and color when he returned to the task of representing his "hallucinations." The sharp precision of form and composition in *The Harlequin's Carnival* was largely given up for bigger and simpler shapes with wavering contours, more loosely arranged, as in *Man Throwing a Stone at a Bird* (Plate 63). The new style achieved a sense of exploration, accident and surprise that enabled Miró to show the dynamics, as well as the substance of subconscious levels of mental life.

"Halluci- nations"

Again, this feature of Miró's art may be contrasted with that of Dali, who proceeds by means of a meticulous and sophisticated realism to analyse the topography of his subconscious in a way that freezes his dreams within the framework of traditional space and sculptural form, thus creating a sense of catastrophe in the fusion of normal and abnormal worlds. Miró does not analyse his secret thoughts in this critical and pessimistic way. Rather, he lets us observe the unfolding of an inner storehouse of mythic symbols by surrendering to the basic, playful impulse of creativity, which finds expression in the interweaving of two-dimensional patterns and images, traced by a wandering line, and filled in with the jewel-like colors of innocence and joy. His method owes much to the inspiration of Paul Klee. But where the Swiss artist makes us feel, in every picture, the delicate vibrations of a spirit probing new and uncertain ground, as he weaves his subtle and complex pictorial textures, in Miró we have the strong repetition and firmness of design that suggests an inner certainty of contact with simple and universal principles, enabling him to transcend personal values, and achieve monumental form.

Contrast with Dali, Klee

Once Miró had achieved this vision and method, he embarked on series after series of great paintings exploring new themes and ideas. Among them were the dream versions of seventeenth-century Dutch domestic interiors from 1928 (Plate 65); the collages and imaginary portraits of the following year (Plate 66); the large abstract works, from 1933 onward, which incorporate words and forms that glow against dark backgrounds (Plate 74); the landscapes with grotesque figures, dating from 1936 (Plate 68); and the savage and tragic works expressing his anguish over the Spanish Civil War (Plates 69, 71). The year 1944 saw the first of the exquisite "constellations" (Plate 76) and the beginning of his work in ceramics (Plates 90, 91, 92); while after the war Miró produced some splendid mural decorations, like the ceramic walls at Unesco headquarters in Paris (Plate 87).

A sense of wonder and unfailing freshness of vision have now become second nature with Miró. He no longer has to try to lose himself in hallucination as he works. Instead he concentrates on exploring the way the forms of his art can grow out of the experience of handling his materials, paint, clay, or print-making processes. This had added a new dimension to his latest works (Plates 81, 88, 89), where the rough and accidental texture of the material world itself provides the design of his dreams.

PAUL H. WALTON

13

FURTHER READING

Salvador Dali, *Diary of a Genius*. New York, 1965.

Salvador Dali, *The Secret Life of Salvador Dali*. New York, 1961.

Robert Descharnes, *The World of Salvador Dali*. New York, 1962.

A. Reynolds Morse, *Dali, A Study of His Life and Work*. New York, 1958.

James Thrall Soby, *Salvador Dali*. New York, 1946.

Jacques Dupin, *Joan Miró, Life and Work*. London, 1962.

Clement Greenberg, *Joan Miró*. New York, 1948.

Sam Hunter, *Joan Miró, His Graphic Work*. New York, 1958.

James Thrall Soby, *Joan Miró*. New York, 1959.

SALVADOR DALI

1904   Born in Figueras, Spain, the son of a notary.

1918   Sees Impressionist and Pointillist painting and begins to practice art seriously.

1921   Enters the Madrid School of Fine Arts.

1923   Influenced by the "Metaphysical" painting of Giorgio de Chirico.

1924   Opposes the administration of the Art School and is suspended for a year.

1925   His paintings begin to be exhibited and he attracts attention for his talent.

1926   Expelled from the Madrid School of Fine Arts for insubordination; experiments with realistic, cubist, and classical styles in his painting.

1927   Begins to produce pictures derived from dream imagery and the symbolism of the unconscious.

1928   First visit to Paris; meets Picasso, André Breton, and the Surrealists.

1929   Returns to Spain and stays in the village of Cadaques trying to provoke symptoms of madness in order to paint visions; here he is visited by some Surrealists, including Eluard the poet, and Gala, his wife; Dali and Gala fall in love; paints his "Invisible Man," the first of his "paranoiac" double images; his first Paris exhibition is held; works on the film *Un Chien Andalou* with Bunuel.

1930 Publishes his first book, *La Femme Visible*.

1931 Works on another film, *L'Age d'Or*, with Bunuel; paints *Persistence of Memory* and begins a series of works dealing with the myth of William Tell.

1934 First exhibition in London, where he gives a famous lecture in a diving suit; first visit to the U.S.A.

1937 First visits to Italy.

1939 Meets Freud in London; designs an amusement pavilion at the New York World's Fair.

1940 Moves to California; breaks with Breton and the Surrealists.

1941 Announces that he intends to become classical in his art; begins a series of portrait commissions; large retrospective exhibition at The Museum of Modern Art in New York.

1942 Publishes his autobiography, *The Secret Life of Salvador Dali*.

1944 Publishes a novel, *Hidden Faces*.

1948 *Leda Atomica* is exhibited, marking the climax of Dali's classicism.

1950 Becomes interested in nuclear physics; his first religious painting is exhibited, *The Madonna of Port Lligat*, and this is the beginning of a continuing series of large scale works.

1951 Living at Port Lligat in Spain.

| 1955 | Delivers a lecture on rhinoceros horns at the Sorbonne. |
| 1964 | Publishes his *Diary of a Genius*. |

JOAN MIRÓ

1893	Born in Barcelona, the son of a goldsmith and jeweller.
1907	Admitted to the St. Luke School of Painting in Barcelona.
1910	His parents compel him to break off his art studies and work in an office.
1912	Takes up art again at the Gali School of Applied Design in Barcelona.
1915	Leaves school to begin his independent career as an artist.
1917	Meets José Dalmau, retired painter and art dealer who champions young artists and progressive art in Barcelona.
1918	Dalmau gives him his first one-man exhibition.
1919	Moves to Paris and becomes friendly with Picasso; shortly afterwards he becomes interested in the Dada movement.
1921	First one-man exhibition in Paris; returns to Spain to live in Montroig; begins *The Farm*.

1925	Second one-man exhibition in Paris; his reputation is established, and he takes part in the first Surrealist exhibition; designs ballet costumes for Diaghilev.
1928	Trip to Holland; on his return begins the series of Dutch interiors.
1930	Begins to make Surrealist sculpture, and undertakes book illustration for the first time, producing color lithographs for Tzara's *L'Arbre des Voyageurs*.
1933	First exhibition in London.
1937	Contributes a painting called *The Reaper* (now lost) to the Spanish Pavilion at the Paris World's Fair which joined with Picasso's *Guernica* in pictorial protest about the Spanish Civil War.
1940	Moves to Palma di Mallorca.
1942	Begins to work in ceramics with the potter Artigas.
1944	Executes fifty lithographs called the *Barcelona Suite*.
1946	Takes up sculpture with increasing enthusiasm.
1947	Makes his first trip to the U.S.A.
1947–48	Executes a large wall painting for a Cincinnati hotel; moves to Montroig and makes frequent visits to Paris.
1950	Publishes a set of 72 color lithographs illustrating Tristan Tzara's *Parler Seul*.

1953   Begins a series of about two hundred ceramics with Artigas.

1956   Builds a large studio at Palma di Mallorca.

1958   Publishes illustrations for Eluard's *A Toute Épreuve;* completes the ceramic walls for UNESCO headquarters.

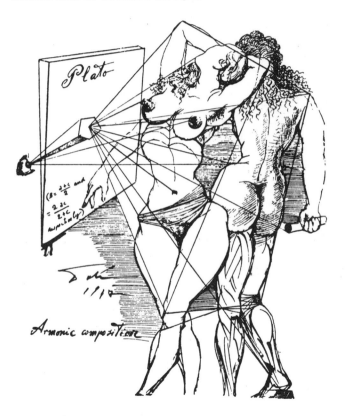

LIST OF COLOR PLATES

SALVADOR DALI

1. Self-Portrait. 1921.
2. Crepuscular Old Man. 1918.
3. Harlequin. 1927.
4. Senecitas. 1926–27.
5. The Invisible Man. 1929–33.
6. Accommodations of Desire. 1929.
7. The Persistence of Memory. 1931.
8. Old Age of William Tel!. 1931.
9. Birth of Liquid Desires. 1932.
10. The Average Fine and Invisible Harp. 1932.
11. The Weaning of Furniture-Nutrition (detail).
12. The Ghost of Vermeer of Delft, Which Can Be Used As a Table. 1934.
13. The Enigma of William Tell. 1934.
14. The Spectre of Sex Appeal. 1934.
15. Archaeological Reminiscence of Millet's Angelus. 1935.
16. Portrait of Gala. 1935.
17. Cavalier of Death. c.1935.
18. Autumn Cannibalism. 1936–37.
19. Venus de Milo of the Drawers. 1936.
20. Perspectives. 1936–37.
21. The Metamorphosis of Narcissus. 1936–37.
22. Impressions of Africa. 1938–39.
23. Slave Market with Invisible Bust of Voltaire. 1940.
24. Portrait of Picasso. 1943.
25. One Second Before Awakening from a Dream Caused by the Flight of a Bee Around a Pomegranate. 1944.
26. The Basket of Bread. 1945.
27. Apotheosis of Homer. 1945.
28. The Madonna of Port Lligat. 1950.
29. Leda Atomica. 1948.
30. The Landscape of Port Lligat. 1950.
31. Gala's Back. 1950.
32. Raphaelesque Head Exploding. 1951.
33. Christ of St. John of the Cross. 1951.
34. Nuclear Cross. 1952.
35. Assumpta Corpuscularia Lapislazulina. 1952.
36. The Maximum Speed of Raphael's Madonna. 1954.
37. The Disintegration of the Persistence of Memory. 1952–54.
38. Sacrament of the Last Supper. 1955.
39. Young Virgin Auto-Sodomized by Her Own Chastity. 1954.

JOAN MIRÓ

NOTES ON THE COLOR PLATES

SALVADOR DALI. PLATES 1–46.

1. *Self-portrait*. 1921. *Oil*. Collection of the Artist. The dark tone, furious brushwork, and dramatic lighting of this sketch, executed while Dali was an art student in Madrid, produce an image of youthful genius recalling the spirit of nineteenth-century Romanticism.

2. *Crepuscular Old Man*. 1918. Oil. Barcelona, Private Collection. Arbitrary incrustations of thick pigment give an individual expressionistic accent to Dali's treatment of a subject that could have been inspired by works from Picasso's "Blue" Period.

3. *Harlequin*. 1927. Oil. Spain, Private Collection. From the beginning of Dali's career as an exhibiting artist, this work was also painted under the influence of Picasso; but this time it is Synthetic Cubism that inspires a huge and sinister head six feet high, one half of which is painted in *trompe l'oeil* imitation of crumpled paper fastened to the canvas in the manner of *papier collé*.

4. *Senecitas*. 1926–27. Oil on panel. Private Collection. An amoeba-like form with a disquieting resemblance to a mutilated torso, pecked at by birds and sprouting red filaments, dominates an early assemblage of anatomical fragments, beasts, and fetish objects dredged from Dali's subconscious, under the influence of Freudian psychology.

5. *The Invisible Man*. 1929–33. Oil. Collection of the Artist. When Dali's dream landscapes begin to be more carefully organized with the aid of architecture, the influence of the Italian forerunner of Surrealism, Giorgio de Chirico, can be detected.

6. *Accommodations of Desire*. 1929. Oil. California, Private Collection. In one of Dali's comments on the cruelty of sex, we see pebbles on the beach near his home in Spain grown into boulders and imprinted with a lion's head in different stages of completion, echoing the savagery of the man-lion embracing a woman in the background.

7. *The Persistence of Memory*. 1931. Oil. New York, Museum of Modern Art. One of Dali's most famous inventions, the soft watches in a dream landscape may suggest the irrational flexibility of dream time, as opposed to the mechanical regularity of normal time.

8. *Old Age of William Tell*. 1931. Oil. Paris, Private Collection. In Dali's art and writings the legend of William Tell is a Freudian allegory of conflict with his own father. The lion, seen in Plate 6, reappears as a shadow symbolizing his father's departed vigor, standing watch over the anguished embrace of a young couple.

9. *Birth of Liquid Desires*. 1932. Oil. Venice, Peggy Guggenheim Collection. Another embracing couple, this time old and hideous, placed before a strange shape resembling a distorted artist's palette, which opens to receive the defeated figure of a younger man. This suggests another comment on Dali's conflict with his father.

10. *The Average Fine and Invisible Harp*. 1932. Oil. Paris, Private Collection. A view of the fishing village of Port Lligat, Dali's home in Spain, where the fantastic hydrocephalic man in the foreground, whose head might break at any moment like the shattered jar he holds, suggests Dali's intense anxiety at this time for the security of his own mind.

11. *The Weaning of Furniture-Nutrition (detail)*. Oil. Cleveland, Morse Collection. The figure on the beach is Dali's nurse, mending nets at Port Lligat. The cabinets and bottle extracted from her torso refer to Dali's dream-memory of the nutrition that he drew from her body, a reminiscence that opens a window on scenes of childhood happiness.

12. *The Ghost of Vermeer of Delft, Which Can Be Used As a Table.* 1934. Oil. Cleveland, Ohio, Morse Collection. The famous self-portrait by Vermeer of Delft, one of Dali's favorite painters, is translated to Port Lligat and transformed into a table offering the wine of his genius to the next passerby, who will be Dali.

13. *The Enigma of William Tell.* 1934. Oil. Stockholm, National Museum. This grotesque father image, his extruded flesh supported on crutches, Dali's favorite fetish, pierces himself with knives in expiation for the act which most people regard as heroic, but which Dali interperted as an assault on his own son.

14. *The Spectre of Sex Appeal.* 1934. Oil. Collection of the Artist. Dali shows himself as a child of six on the beach at Port Lligat, confronting a monstrous apparition displaying the horror of female flesh, which adult appetites can imbue with desirability.

15. *Archaeological Reminiscence of Millet's Angelus.* 1935. Oil on panel. Cleveland, Morse Collection. The central figures from Millet's famous painting become gigantic ruins, visited in the desert by travellers. Dali's own archaeological excavation of this monument with Freudian tools resulted in his discovery that the figures show symptoms of sexual repression and guilt.

16. *Portrait of Gala.* 1935. Oil. New York, Museum of Modern Art. Seen from behind, Dali's wife confronts herself seated in a wheelbarrow before a version of Millet's *Angelus,* where the figures are also seated on a wheelbarrow, ·which is, for Dali, a symbol of sexual attraction.

17. *Cavalier of Death.* c. 1935. Oil. Private Collection. In front of a black cliff inspired by the German artist Boecklin's *Island of the Dead,* a popular nineteenth-century painting, Dali places a ghostly horse and rider precariously constructed of bones, rocks, and healthy flesh. The rider can be related to comparable figures by German artists like Dürer and Rethel, so that the picture becomes a kind of tribute to German romanticism.

18. *Autumn Cannibalism.* 1936–37. Oil. London, Tate Gallery. Two figures half-formed of doughy flesh embrace, but at the same time they dig into each other with knife, fork, and spoon in a savage feast of love.

19. *Venus de Milo of the Drawers.* 1936. Plaster. Paris, Private Collection. This plaster version of the Venus de Milo is a variation on one of Dali's most memorable inventions, where the feminine form is combined with a chest of drawers to provide a comment on the symbiotic relationship between human anatomy and furniture, which was invented for the comfort of the body but has become indispensable to its biological functions.

20. *Perspectives.* 1936–37. Oil. Switzerland, Basel Kunstmuseum. Careful study reveals how the tiny figures scattered on the vast plain are grouped in configurations that echo the anguished heads in the foreground.

21. *The Metamorphosis of Narcissus.* 1936–37. Oil. London, Tate Gallery. In the Greek myth Narcissus died admiring himself in a pool of water. Dali shows him changed to rock, like Echo, the nymph he had shunned, and ironically, his form is echoed in the stone hand holding an egg from which the flower sprouts that now bears his name.

22. *Impressions of Africa.* 1938–39. Oil. London, Tate Gallery. In this self-portrait Dali shows himself at his easel, stretching toward us a hand so realistically painted that it seems to project from the canvas; but in the landscape behind him this realism is contradicted by a profusion of double images.

23. *Slave Market with Invisible Bust of Voltaire.* 1940. Ohio, Private Collection. The nude at the left contemplates figures under an arch in the ruined building, and they combine to form a bust of Voltaire on a pedestal on the table.

24. *Portrait of Picasso.* 1943. Oil. Collection of the Artist. Picasso is here subjected to distortions as violent as those he has ever imposed on his models. Is there a note of derision, born of rivalry, in the way Dali shows him presenting a tiny mandolin to the world?

25. *One Second Before Awakening from a Dream Caused by the Flight of a Bee Around a Pomegranate.* 1944. Oil. U.S.A., Private Collection. The pomegranate, a symbol of immortality and fertility, here explodes into a fish disgorging tigers which pounce on a voluptuous nude, Dali's wife. These images and their import may be compared with the work in Plate 6.

26. *The Basket of Bread.* 1945. Oil. Collection of the Artist. A surprising exercise in "magic realism." Dali's bread is also symbolic, having for him a positive value as a sacrament (see Plates 34 and 35), and a negative value as the common staple of the masses that he wished to "cretinize."

27. *Apotheosis of Homer.* 1945. Oil. Paris, Private Collection. An extraordinarily complex dream landscape, with many classical references. This is the last baroque elaboration of the type of painting that Dali developed in the thirties.

28. *The Madonna of Port Lligat.* 1950. Oil. Canada, Private Collection. Combining classicism and religious sentiment in a new manner, this calm and monumental work nevertheless derives from the painting in Plate 11 in its setting, and in the use of windows in the body which here frame the bread of the Eucharist in the exact center of the picture.

29. *Leda Atomica.* 1948. Oil. Collection of the Artist. Dali's wife, Gala, here appears in a classical role in a work painted earlier than the complementary *Madonna of Port Lligat,* where she is shown as the Madonna. From now on Gala is seen very frequently in Dali's work during a period of "Galamania."

30. *The Landscape of Port Lligat.* 1950. Oil. Cleveland, Morse Collection. This realistic painting of the view from Dali's home at Port Lligat reveals a landscape that appears very frequently in his works. The figures on the shore show that for him it is the kind of realm that angels might inhabit.

31. *Gala's Back.* 1950. Oil. Collection of the Artist. Dali's classicism, originating with his trips to Italy from 1937, here leads him to treat the tradi-

tional theme of the idealized female nude in a cool and refined linear style recalling Ingres (cf. Plate 29), and inviting comparison with the *Basket of Bread* (Plate 26), based on the more dramatic Baroque realism of Vermeer.

32. *Raphaelesque Head Exploding.* 1951. Oil. England, Private Collection. An interest in nuclear physics has led Dali to treat a number of themes in terms of exploding particles, like this classical head superimposed on the dome of the Pantheon in Rome, with its circular opening admitting what Dali refers to as "spiritual light."

33. *Christ of St. John of the Cross.* 1951. Oil. Glasgow, Art Gallery and Museum. Strongly foreshortened, like a crucifix inclined toward the worshiper as he kisses it, Christ on the Cross is suspended over the familiar landscape of Port Lligat, with its fishermen and boats, in one of Dali's most dramatic and popular inventions.

34. *Nuclear Cross.* 1952. Oil. Paris, Private Collection. This cross formed of cubes is meant to resemble the elements of an atomic pile centering on the bread of the Eucharist. It expresses Dali's hope for a synthesis of nuclear science and Christian mysticism.

35. *Assumpta Corpuscularia Lapislazulina.* 1952. Oil. Private Collection. Gala appears again as the Virgin, elongated, fragmented, and drawn up to heaven after her death from a globe representing the earth and atom, and superimposed on the Dome of the Pantheon, Christ of St. John of the Cross, and an altar.

36. *The Maximum Speed of Raphael's Madonna.* 1954. Oil. Collection of the Artist. A fragmented version of Raphael's *Madonna del Cardellino* made of atomic particles and the rhinoceros horns, in which Dali believes he discovered in 1955 the secret of curvilinear beauty in classical art.

37. *The Disintegration of the Persistence of Memory.* 1952–54. Oil.

Cleveland, Ohio, Morse Collection. This new version of an earlier work (compare with Plate 7) brings it up to date by employing the blocks of an atomic pile (Plate 34) and the exploded, floating forms of Dali's religious works (Plate 28) to create a complex synthesis of science, dreams and mysticism. The sea is wittily caught up like a sheet on a tree branch at the left.

38. *Sacrament of the Last Supper.* 1955. Oil. Washington, National Gallery. Sunlight streams across the bay at Port Lligat, through the transparent body of Christ as he breaks the bread of the Sacrament and announces "This is my body." At the same time, an apparition of his flesh in the pose of the Crucifixion appears above the bowed heads of the apostles with their modern haircuts. The scene takes place within a structure which Dali describes as "the celestial dodecahedron," expressing the sublimity of twelve, the number of apostles, months, and signs of the zodiac.

39. *Young Virgin Auto-Sodomized by Her Own Chastity.* 1954. Oil. New York, Private Collection. Dali maintains that this combination of a female nude with rhinoceros horns creates an image of innocence, because he associates the rhinoceros horn with the horn of the unicorn, a medieval symbol of chastity.

40. *Nature Morte Vivante.* 1956. Oil. Cleveland, Ohio, Morse Collection. The hand at the left holds a rhinoceros horn beside an assortment of objects that could combine to form a traditional still life. Instead, they float away, and water splashes from the bottle to become involved in the fragmentation of the fruit dish. The round form at the right is a cauliflower, which Dali uses as a symbol of beauty, because he associates it with the texture of rhinoceros hide and the beautiful curve of the horn.

41. *Study of Vermeer's Lacemaker.* 1955. Oil. Private Collection. Dali's version of a seventeenth-century masterpiece by the Dutch artist Vermeer was the result of his study of the rhinoceros horn as the key to visual beauty. Here he emphasizes his discovery of its shape in Vermeer's painting in "a restless rearrangement of the static elements of the original," where only a face is immediately recognizable, just above the center of the composition.

42. *Saint Surrounded by Three Pi-Mesons.* 1956. Oil. Private Collection. The almost completely abstract assemblage of wildly agitated particles suggests a figure, and represents another attempt by Dali to "unlock the still unknown mystical values that must underlie modern nuclear science."

43. *Santiago El Grande.* 1957. Oil. Canada, Lord Beaverbrook Art Gallery. Dali's largest painting treats St. James, the patron saint of Spain, who was said to have liberated the country from the Moors. He is shown under an intricate Gothic structure, mounted like a military hero on a rearing horse which bears a shell on its chest, symbol of St. James's pilgrimage to Compostella, where a great shrine is dedicated to him. The horse's hind quarters are involved in an atomic cloud, and the saint brandishes a living crucifix (compare with Plate 33) instead of a sword. Below we see the familiar landscape of Port Lligat, with Gala as a shrouded pilgrim.

44. *Ear with Madonna.* 1958. Oil. New York, Museum of Modern Art. The atomic disintegration of the subject is here achieved by means of a screen of dots, in front of which there float two pieces of paper, painted illusionistically. Behind the screen we can make out the Madonna and Child embedded in a huge ear.

45. *Pietà of the Apocalypse of St. John.* 1960. Etching and watercolor. This drawing of Christ mourned by His Mother is almost obscured by an accidental pattern printed on the paper from a copper plate which had been exposed to the explosion of a bomb filled with nails. This is Dali's fantastic version of experiments by contemporary artists with the use of chance as a source of artistic form and inspiration.

46. *The Council.* 1960. Oil. Belgium, Private Collection. Dali's self-portrait is here surrounded by motifs related to many of his later paintings: the rocks of Port Lligat, Gala as a saint, the figures of a martyr in a classical niche. It displays in monumental form the lack of stylistic and thematic unity that has characterized most of Dali's work since about 1940.

47. *Self-Portrait.* 1919. Oil. Picasso Collection. A flattened and angular design directs our eye towards a compact constellation of features staring at us in a way somehow suggesting a face looking through a porthole, to give a vivid suggestion of a soul contacting us from within the body. Note the evocative repetitions in the pattern of the shirt collar, head, and hair.

48. *Fruit and Bottle.* 1915. Oil. Private Collection. The impulsive rhythms and rough paint texture in this work show Miró responding to the influence of Matisse and the Fauve group of painters in Paris. ·

49. *The Path, Ciurana.* 1917. Oil. Paris, Private Collection. In a tightly interlocking arrangement of flat patterns suggested by roads, fields, trees and hills, Miró creates a landscape jumping with the convulsive visual energy of Fauve art.

50. *Portrait of E. C. Ricart.* 1917. Oil. Chicago, Private Collection. The heavy black contours and changing colors in this portrait stand out against the delicate line and flat tints of a Japanese print pasted on the canvas. The contrast underlines Miró's "modernity," for his figure makes this kind of print, once the talisman of avant-garde painting, appear restrained and traditional.

51. *Still Life with Coffee Mill.* 1918. Oil. Paris, Galerie Maeght. The repetition of overlapping planes and angles in this still life, together with the inclusion of a ticket, pasted on the canvas in the manner of the collages invented by Picasso and Braque, show Miró's awareness of cubist ideas even before his first visit to Paris.

52. *Seated Nude.* 1919. Oil. New York, Private Collection. The colorful patterns of the striped rug and petit point on the stool combine rather uneasily with the transparent planes in the analytic cubism of the figure.

53. *View of Montroig*. 1919. Oil. Paris, Galerie Maeght. The old walls of Miró's native village, raked by a high, hot sun, are treated with loving realism, but the fields and trees are given cubist complexities of geometric organization.

54. *The Farm*. 1921–22. Oil. Havana, Hemingway Collection. The subject-matter is much the same as in the previous work, but remnants of realistic light and atmosphere are given up, as well as Fauve looseness of movement, in favor of rigid geometry and the crystallization of every form into a flat, emblematic shape. The vivid contrast of primary colors with black and white give a symbolic rendition of the heat, light, and red earth characteristic of Miró's Spanish home.

55. *The Carbide Lamp*. 1922–23. Oil. New York, Museum of Modern Art. The stark simplicity of this design, with its realistic rendition of a machine object, recalls the cubist purism of Juan Gris, and the mechanical subject matter of Léger. It forms a contrast with the complexities of *The Farm*.

56. *The Harlequin's Carnival*. 1924–25. Oil. Buffalo, Albright Art Gallery. A comparison between this surrealist interior, and the "primitive" landscape called *The Farm* (Plate 54) is rewarding. In the latter, note the white s-curved path, the ladder, the tiny child squatting on the ground, and the repeated circles of the sun and earth. These forms reappear in the work as snake shapes, a walking ladder, a dancing cat in the foreground, and assorted heads and balls. Similar correspondences and repetitions are found throughout Miró's work, giving it unity of meaning and form.

57. *Maternity*. 1924. Oil. London, Penrose Collection. Simple shapes and spidery lines here suggest breasts, embryos, and a pubic triangle, to produce a diagrammatic fertility symbol.

58. *Woman, Journal and Dog*. 1925. Oil. Paris, Private Collection. See Note 61.

59. *Head of a Catalan Peasant.* 1925. Oil. Stockholm, Private Collection.

60. *The Siesta.* 1925. Oil. Paris, Private Collection. See Note 61.

61. *Painting.* 1925. Oil. Barcelona, Private Collection. From 1925 to 1927 Miró produced a number of more abstract paintings where thin lines and flat colors hesitantly trace elementary designs like children's scribbles on a surface that is often freely brushed with an electric blue. These were done as "automatic" paintings, without conscious control, and they may incorporate numbers, letters or words, in compositions that poignantly suggest the first formation of conceptual order out of chaos.

62. *Dog Barking at the Moon.* 1926. Oil. Philadelphia Museum of Art. With new-found economy of means Miró here gives us a charming fairy tale fantasy. A multi-hued ladder reaches from the red earth up into the night, watched with equal dismay by the dog and swift sailing moon, both humorously twisted in shape and gaily colored.

63. *Man Throwing a Stone at a Bird.* 1926. Oil. Philadelphia Museum of Art. Two elemental life forms confront each other in a stark beach setting in a painting that is like a diagram of how the first missile was thrown—adding new elements of surprise and danger to the hunt.

64. *Object.* 1931. Painted wood with feather and metals. France, Private Collection. The appearance of child-like spontaneity and accident in this gay surrealist construction is combined with an underlying wit, control and poetry possible only to a mature artist.

65. *Dutch Interior.* 1928. Oil. Chicago, Private Collection. A realistic Dutch painting has provided the initial stimulus for a free fantasy in Miró's private language of shape and color. Comparison between the original and Miró's version produces a reaction exactly the opposite to the one that would be created by a perfectly faithful imitation. Here we are amazed that the artist can be so independent in his interpretation, with changes of emphasis and scale

that demonstrate his truly astonishing freedom in his art from the material interests of realistic painting, and those who like it.

66. *Collage, Summer*. 1929. Paper and wire. Paris, Private Collection. See Note 70.

67. *Painting*. 1930. Oil. U.S.A., Private Collection. See Note 70.

68. *Personages, Mountains, Star and Bird*. 1936. Tempera. Paris, Private Collection. The wit and gaiety of works like *The Harlequin's Carnival* (Plate 56) here gives way to a more savage mood in the depiction of what could be an extra-terrestrial landscape where grotesque creatures roam and glare at us in a threatening way that suggests the influence of Miró's friend Salvador Dali.

69. *Still Life with Old Shoe*. 1937. Oil. U.S.A., Private Collection. The objects shown here are an apple impaled by a fork, a gin bottle partly wrapped in paper, a loaf of bread, and an old shoe. These symbols of poverty, depicted with a new degree of realism, are given monumental dignity amidst enveloping black shadows shot through with lurid colors. This is Miró's comment on the suffering of the people of Spain during the Civil War.

70. *Gouache on Black Paper*. 1937. Gouache. See also Plates 66, 67. In these works planetary shapes and nebulous colors drift in a featureless void like celestial phenomena, suggesting a connection with Miró's youthful interest in amateur astronomy.

71. *Head of a Woman*. 1938. Oil. Los Angeles, Private Collection. Like a victim of the Spanish War transformed by fear into a monster, a savage figure throws up her arms and snarls with rage at her tormentors. This violent painting invites comparison with the way Picasso depicted the horror of the war in his *Guernica*.

72. *Woman in Front of the Sun*. 1938. Oil. New York, Private Collection.

Another woman with upflung arms, but this time the creative power of a blazing sun dispels the smoke of war in a more hopeful image.

73. *The Ladder of Escape*. 1939. Oil. Chicago, Private Collection.

74. *Snail, Woman, Flower, Star*. 1934. Oil. Spain, Private Collection.

75. *Personages in the Night Guided by the Phosphorescent Tracks of Snails*. 1940. Oil and gouache. New York, Private Collection. In 1933 Miró began to produce this distinctive and poetic kind of painting where forms, and sometimes words, are drawn over flat areas of color and texture with a flowing line that transforms his favorite monsters, moons, stars, and embryonic shapes into decorative patterns. Areas created by the intersecting lines are filled in by what might be called checkerboard patterns of vivid color, which may glow with fiery luminosity against dark backgrounds. These are among Miró's most exuberant creations, with their suggestion of the free flight of the artist's hand and imagination, traced by a moving line that spontaneously generates surprising shapes and patterns as it goes.

76. *Woman Encircled by the Flight of a Bird*. 1940. Gouache. Paris, Private Collection. This is one of a series of paintings produced in 1940 which Miró called "constellations." They are a development of the style in the preceding three plates, but more abstract and intricate, smaller in scale, and more carefully pondered in terms of compositional balance.

77. *Woman and Bird in Front of the Sun*. 1944. Oil. Genoa, Private Collection.

78. *Painting*. 1944. Oil. Barcelona, Private Collection.

79. *Woman and Bird in Front of the Sun*. 1944. Oil. Canada, Private Collection. In 1945 many of Miró's paintings began to be dominated by boldly brushed motifs combining suggestions of animal and alphabet forms. These in-

dicate a new interest in the runic signs and ideograms that for primitive peoples were imbued with mystery and magic power.

80. *Acrobats in the Night Garden*. 1948. Lithograph. See Note 82.

81. *Composition*. 1950. Oil. The Netherlands, Eindhoven Art Gallery. This painting shows a new feature of much of Miró's work after 1950. The accidental smears and patches of color, which in earlier works were muted to provide a background for his designs, now become stronger in tone and contrast, pressing forward to compete with the drawing for our attention. This is the result of Miró's increasing concern to let accidental textures suggest, and become part of his compositions.

82. *The Bird Catchers*. 1950. Lithograph. See also Plate 80. Since World War II Miró has been exploring the resources of various print-making techniques. These early lithographs show him delighting in the dazzling contrast between white paper and pure color in sequences of ideogrammatic forms and scribbles that have a somewhat experimental character.

83. *Series I*. 1952–53. Etching.

84. *Composition*. 1953. Etching. In the 1950's Miró began to use etching and aquatint to produce color prints. These two examples show him exploiting the possibility offered by aquatint to create grainy background textures to set off symbol-creatures that have now become more rough and forceful in definition than the first generation of ideograms from the forties (compare with Plate 78).

85. *The Sad Wanderer*. 1955. Lithograph.

86. *The Sun Eater*. 1955. Lithograph. These later lithographs are more monumental and unified in composition than those of the previous decade (Plates 80, 82).

87. *The Sun Wall* (above). *The Moon Wall* (below). 1955-58. Ceramic. Paris, UNESCO Headquarters. Commissioned for UNESCO Headquarters in Paris, these murals are built of ceramic slabs attached to free standing walls built in the square in front of the building. Miró has said that he sought "a brutal expression in the large wall, a more poetic one in the smaller," and at the same time he wanted to create a contrast with the concrete block of the building that would humanize it, and make it part of nature. The walls took four years to complete, with the aid of José Artigas, an expert potter.

88. *Joy of a Little Girl in Front of the Sun.* 1960. Oil. Private Collection.

89. *The Red Disk.* 1960. Oil. New York, Private Collection. These recent paintings show combinations of bold graphic forms and accidental textures that are perfectly in tune with contemporary interests in chance as an element in art forms like action painting, aleatory music, and happenings.

90. *Ceramic* (above). 1955. Paris, Galerie Maeght. *The Face* (below). 1956. Ceramic.

91. *Composition.* Ceramic. Private Collection.

92. *Composition* (above). Ceramic. Private Collection. *Composition* (below). Ceramic. Private Collection. Miró's recent ceramics are also frequently suggested by chance configurations of the clay, and he then cooperates with nature by adding glazes and graphic elements. Working with the aid of Artigas, Miró has thus extended his art decisively into the third dimension, again showing himself a leader in the most recent trend away from the limitations of the easel painting.

THE PLATES

1
Dali: *Self-Por-trait*. 1921. Oil.
18¾ × 12¼ in.
Collection of the
Artist. The viewer
is transfixed by a
piercing gaze.

2
Dali: *Crepuscular Old Man*. 1918. Oil. Barcelona, Private Collection. An expressionist theme— the tragedy of old age.

3 Dali: *Harlequin*. 1927. Oil. 74¾ × 55⅛ in. Barcelona, Private Collection. This clown is uncanny rather than gay.

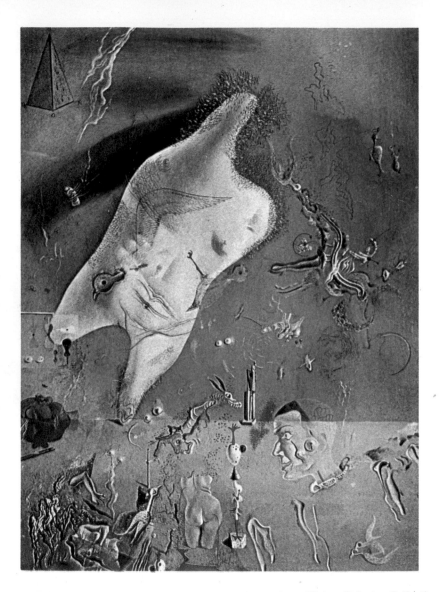

4 Dali: *Senecitas*. 1926–27. Oil on panel. 25⅛ × 18⅞ in. Private Collection. The debris of the unconscious floats into Dali's art.

5 Dali: *The Invisible Man*. 1929–33. Oil. 55⅛ × 31½ in. Collection of the Artist. His own
existence seems to take him by surprise.

6 Dali: *Accommodations of Desire*. 1929. Oil. 8⅝ × 13¾ in. California, Private Collection.
The lion's head was cut from a magazine and attached to the canvas.

7 Dali: *The Persistence of Memory*. 1931. Oil. 9½ × 13 in. New York, Museum of Modern Art. Dali says the softness of these watches was inspired by his love of Camembert cheese.

8 Dali: *Old Age of William Tell*. 1931. Oil. 38½ × 55⅛ in. Paris, Private Collection. A shadow threatens lovers in a landscape.

9 Dali: *Birth of Liquid Desires*. 1932. Oil. 38⅜ × 44½ in. Venice, Peggy Guggenheim Collection. The rock-like forms flow and melt.

10
Dali: *The
Average Fine
and Invisible
Harp*. 1932.
Oil. Paris,
Private Col-
lection. The
impossible be-
comes photo-
graphically
real.

11 Dali: *The Weaning of Furniture-Nutrition* (detail). Oil. 7¼ × 9½ in. Cleveland, Morse Collection. This grandmother has strange children!

12   Dali: *The Ghost of Vermeer of Delft, Which Can Be Used As a Table.* 1934. Oil. 7¼ × 5½ in.
Cleveland, Morse Collection.   The table and the waiter are one.

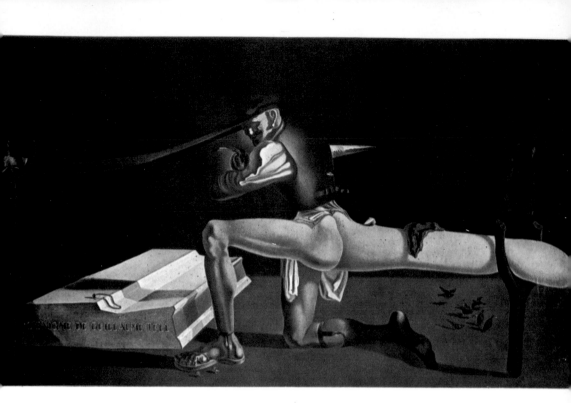

13 Dali: *The Enigma of William Tell.* 1934. Oil. 78¾ × 128 in. Stockholm, National Museum.
William Tell cradles the infant Dali in his arms.

14 Dali: *The Spectre of Sex Appeal*. 1934. Oil. 7¼ × 5½ in. Collection of the Artist. A nightmare in miniature.

15 Dali: *Archaeological Reminiscence of Millet's Angelus*. **1935.** Oil on panel. **12½ × 15⅜** in. Cleveland, Morse Collection. The metamorphosis of figures into ruins.

16 Dali: *Portrait of Gala*. 1935. Oil. 12⅝ × 10¼ in. New York, Museum of **Modern Art**. The face is rendered with cruel truthfulness.

17 Dali: *Cavalier of Death.*   c. 1935.   Oil.   16 × 12 in.   Private Collection.   The rider is himself overtaken by decay.

18 Dali: *Autumn Cannibalism*. 1936–37. Oil. 31½ × 31½ in. London, Tate Gallery. The landscape is also a kitchen table.

19 Dali: *Venus de Milo of the Drawers*. 1936. Plaster. h. 39⅜ in. Paris, Private Collection.
A clock in the stomach would be no less strange.

20 Dali: *Perspectives.* 1936–37. Oil. 25⅝ × 25¾ in. Switzerland, Basel Kunstmuseum.
Strangely purposeful figures populate this desert.

21 Dali: *The Metamorphosis of Narcissus*. 1936–37. Oil. 20⅛ × 29⅞ in. London, Tate Gallery.
Dali took this painting to his famous meeting with Freud.

22 Dali: *Impressions of Africa.* 1938–39. Oil. 36 × 50 in. London, Tate Gallery. Dali remembers Africa, but has never been there!

23   Dali: *Slave Market with Invisible Bust of Voltaire*.   1940.   Oil.   18¼ × 25¾ in.   Ohio, Private Collection.   This double image exemplifies the artist's "paranoiac-critical" method.

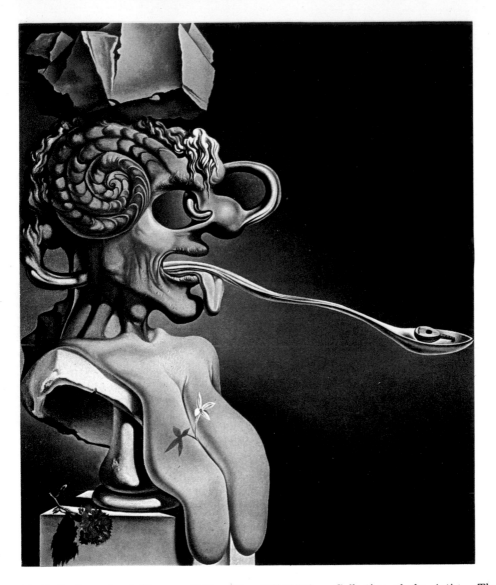

24 Dali: *Portrait of Picasso*. 1943. Oil. 26¼ × 22 in. Collection of the **Artist**. The brain shapes itself into a spoon.

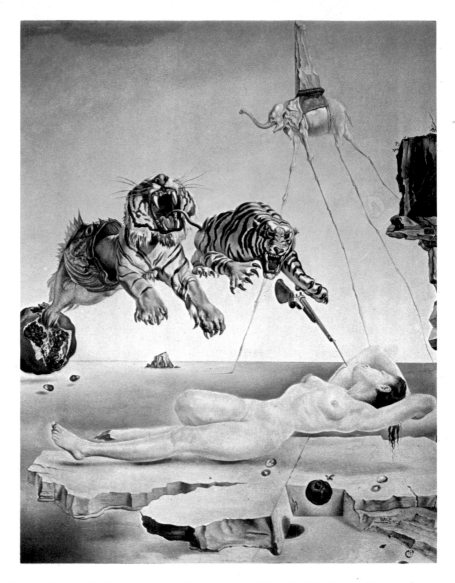

25 Dali: *One Second Before Awakening from a Dream Caused by the Flight of a Bee Around a Pomegranate*. 1944. Oil. 20⅛ × 15⅞ in. U.S.A., Priv. Coll. Every object floats in space.

26 Dali: *The Basket of Bread.* 1945. Oil. 13 × 14⅞ in. Collection of the Artist. In Dali's art, truth seems strange when it appears.

27 Dali: *Apotheosis of Homer*. 1945. Oil. 25⅛ × 46 in. Paris, Private Collection. A junkyard
of discarded dreams.

28 Dali: *The Madonna of Port Lligat*. 1950. Oil. 142⅜ × 96 in. Canada, Private Collection.
New elements appear, piety and symmetry.

29 Dali: *Leda Atomica*. 1948. Oil. 18⅞ × 24⅜ in. Collection of the Artist. Even the sea is detached from the shore.

30 Dali: *The Landscape of Port Lligat*. 1950. Oil. 23 × 31⅜ in. Cleveland, Morse Collection. A loving rendition of the view from Dali's Spanish home.

31 Dali: *Gala's Back*. 1950. Oil. 16⅞ × 12⅝ in. Collection of the Artist. This study is unfinished.

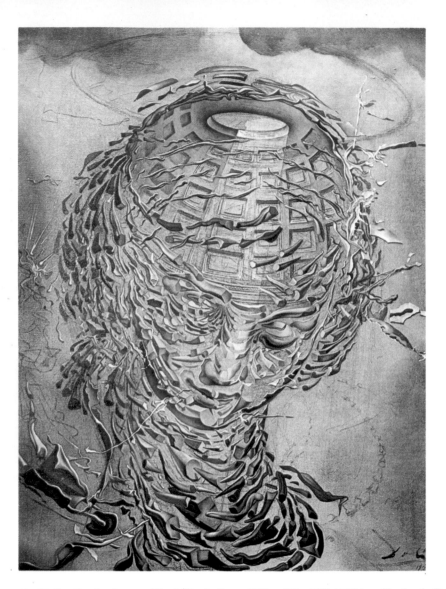

32 Dali: *Raphaelesque Head Exploding.* 1951. Oil. 16⅞ × 13 in. England, Private Collection.
The wheelbarrow at lower left is a favorite fetish.

33
Dali: *Christ of St. John of the Cross.* 1951. Oil. 80¾ × 45⅝ in. Glasgow, Art Gallery and Museum. This is Dali's challenge to Renaissance masters of anatomy and perspective.

34 Dali: *Nuclear Cross*. 1952. Oil. 30¾ × 22⅞ in. Paris, Private Collection. The bread of the Eucharist shines like the moon.

35
Dali: *Assumpta
Corpuscularia
Lapislazulina.* 1952.
Oil. 90¼ × 56¾ in.
Private Collection.
Gala reappears as
the Virgin.

← 36 Dali: *The Maximum Speed of Raphael's Madonna*. 1954. Oil. 32 × 26 in. Collection of the Artist. An atomic reinterpretation of a monument of Renaissance classicism.

37 Dali: *The Disintegration of the Persistence of Memory*. 1952–54. Oil. 10 × 13 in. Cleveland, Morse Collection. Dali's post-war optimism is here conveyed by a cheerful harmony of blue and orange.

38
Dali:
Sacrament of the Last Supper.
1955. Oil.
66 ×
113 in.
Washington,
National
Gallery.
The apostles are
disposed
with perfect symmetry.

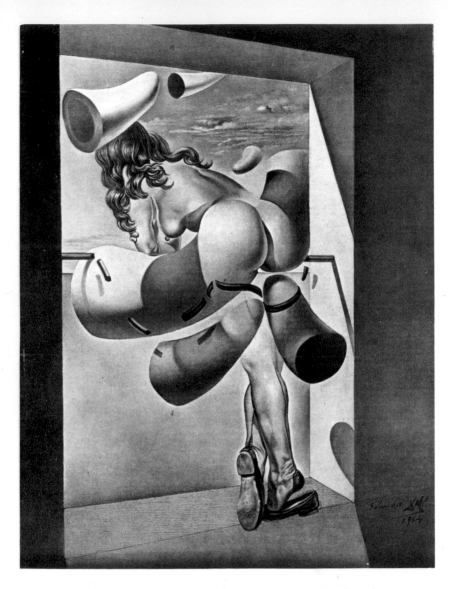

39 Dali: *Young Virgin Auto-Sodomized by Her Own Chastity*. 1954. Oil. 15⅞ × 12 in. New York, Private Collection. Her room overlooks the Mediterranean.

40 Dali: *Nature Morte Vivante*. 1956. Oil. 49½ × 64⅛ in. Cleveland, Morse Collection. In front of the same sea the artist paints an animated still life.

41 Dali: *Study of Vermeer's Lacemaker*. 1955. Oil. 9½ × 8¼ in. Private Collection. Dali
shows a Dutch masterpiece exploding into rhinoceros horns.

42 Dali: *Saint Surrounded by Three Pi-Mesons*. 1956. Oil. 16¾ ×11¾ in. Private Collection. The saint is shown as a shower of glittering atomic particles.

43 Dali: *Santiago El Grande*. 1957. Oil. 157½ × 118⅛ in. Canada, Beaverbrook Art Gallery. The artist gives us a grandiose vision of a Christian hero.

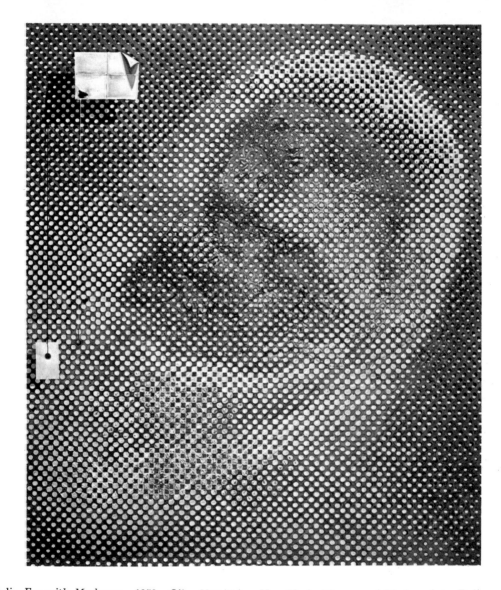

44 Dali: *Ear with Madonna.* 1958. Oil. 88 × 75 in. New York, Museum of Modern Art. Dali teases the eye in a new way.

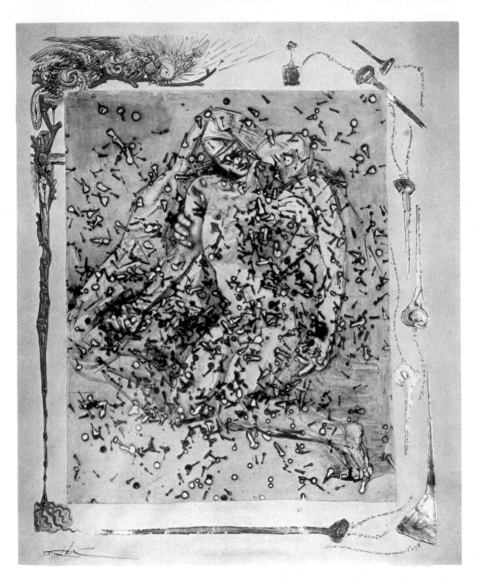

45 Dali: *Pietà of the Apocalypse of St. John.* 1962. Etching and watercolor. 22⅞ × 18⅛ in. An image of death and destruction is given a precious border decoration.

46 Dali: *The Council*. 1960. Oil. 157½ × 118⅛ in. Belgium, Private Collection. Baroque agitation replaces classical calm.

← 47   Miró: *Self-Portrait*. 1919. Oil. Picasso Collection. In an early masterpiece, **Miró combines** geometric stylization, realism, and psychological depth.

48   Miró: *Fruit and Bottle*. 1915. Oil. 18⅞ × 24 in. Private Collection. Dark tones give dignity to the unleashed energy of this expressionistic study.

49 Miró: *The Path, Ciurana.* 1917. Oil. 23⅝ × 28¾ in. Paris, Private Collection. The landscape becomes a bold pattern, almost abstract.

50 Miró: *Portrait of E. C. Ricart.* 1917. Oil. 31⅞ × 25⅝ in. Private Collection. The shape of the palette foreshadows future motifs.

The Very Best Collection of
Souvenir Post Cards
OF NEW YORK CITY

30 FOR **25**c.

THE NOVELTY SHOP

51 Miró: *Still Life with Coffee Mill.* **1918.** Oil. 24⅝ × 27¾ in. Paris, Galerie Maeght. In this experiment with collage, the ticket seems an intrusion.

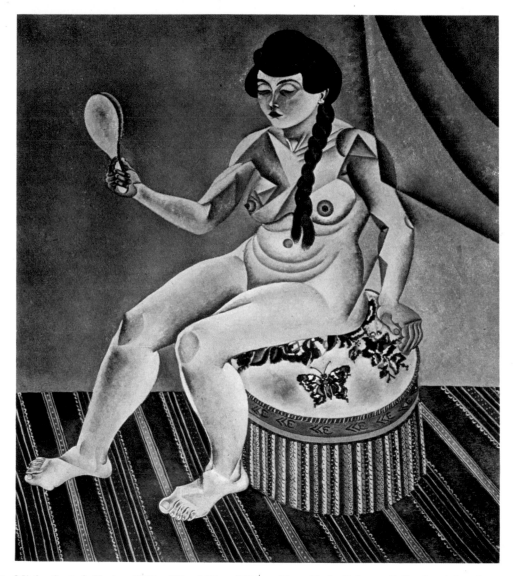

52 Miró: *Seated Nude*. 1919. Oil. 44⅛ × 40⅛ in. New York, Private Collection. A solemn
tribute to Cubism.

53 Miró: *View of Montroig*. 1919. Oil. 28¾ × 24 in. Paris, Galerie Maeght. The contrast between realism and abstraction is very sharp.

54 Miró: *The Farm*. 1921–22. Oil. 52 × 57⅞ in. Havana, Hemıngway Collection. **In this work**
Ernest Hemingway recognized the essence of Spain.

55 Miró: *The Carbide Lamp*. 1922–23. Oil. 15 × 18⅛ in. New York, Museum of Modern Art. Hot metal is the theme of a crisp design.

56 Miró: *The Harlequin's Carnival.* 1924–25. Oil. 26 × 36⅝ in. Buffalo, Albright Art Gallery. Miró's dream-circus is a grotesque and gay entertainment.

57 Miró: *Maternity*. 1924. Oil. 35⅞ × 29⅛ in. London, Penrose Collection. The microscope might reveal forms like these.

58 Miró: *Woman, Journal and Dog*. 1925. Oil. Paris, Private Collection. **A jaunty lady sets out for a walk.**

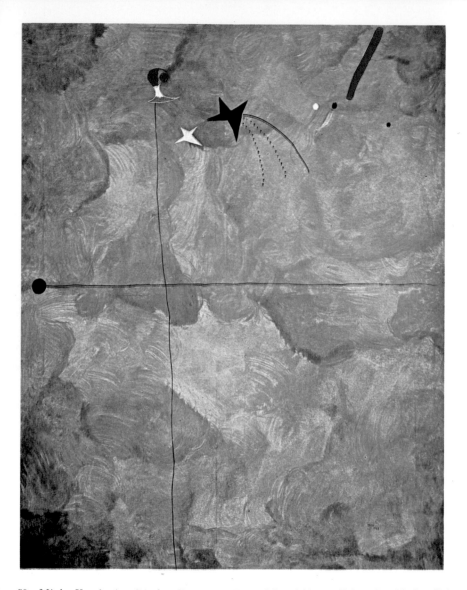

59 Miró: *Head of a Catalan Peasant*. 1925. Oil. $57\frac{1}{2} \times 44\frac{7}{8}$ in. Stockholm, Private Collection.
Form is reduced to its simplest elements.

60 Miró: *The Siesta*. 1925. Oil. 38⅛ × 57½ in. Paris, Private Collection. Recognizable shapes struggle to emerge.

61 Miró: *Painting*. 1925. Oil. 19¼ × 23⅝ in. Barcelona, Private Collection. Random tracks are traced through another dazzling blue field.

62 Miró: *Dog Barking at the Moon*. 1926. Oil. 28¾ × 36¼ in. Philadelphia Museum of Art.
A rainbow ladder reaches for the stars.

Miró: *Man Throwing a Stone at a Bird.* 1926. Oil. 28¾ × 36¼ in. Philadelphia Museum Art. Bright colors and bold shapes create electric excitement.

64 Miró: *Object*. 1931. Painted wood with feather and metals. 44⅞ × 28¾ in. France, Private Coll. This Surrealist construction is an ancestor of works by young artists like Rauschenberg.

65 Miró: *Dutch Interior*. 1928. Oil. 51⅛ × 38⅝ in. Chicago, Private Collection. Miró's version of a realistic painting retains few traces of the original.

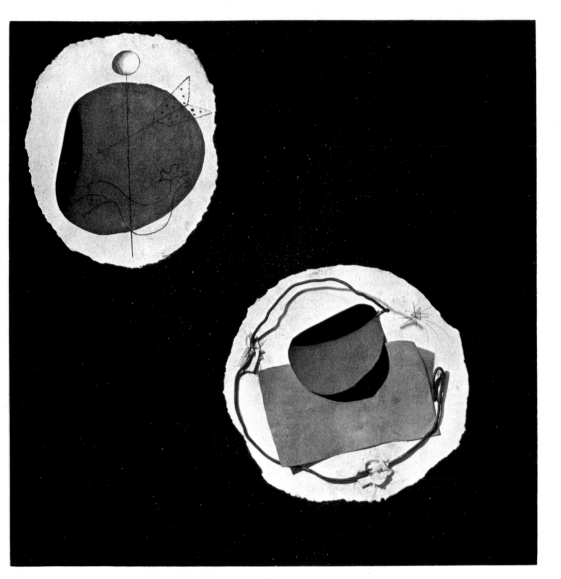

66 Miró: *Collage, Summer.* 1929. Paper and wire. 42⅛ × 42⅛ in. Paris, Private Collection. Scraps from the real world are set afloat in pictorial space.

67   Miró: *Painting*. 1930. Oil. 59 × 88⅝ in. U.S.A., Private Collection. Radical simplicity and monumental scale foretell post-war American abstraction.

68 Miró: *Personages, Mountains, Star and Bird.* **1936.** Tempera. 11⅞ × 15¾ in. Paris, Private Collection. Miró invents new anatomies to create weird inhabitants of a desert world.

69   Miró: *Still Life with Old Shoe*. 1937. Oil. 31⅞ × 45⅝ in. U.S.A., Private Collection. In this still life with a message each object is a symbol of poverty and suffering.

70   Miró: *Gouache on Black Paper*. 1937. Gouache. Private Collection. This astonishingly free and casual abstraction creates a glow of colored light.

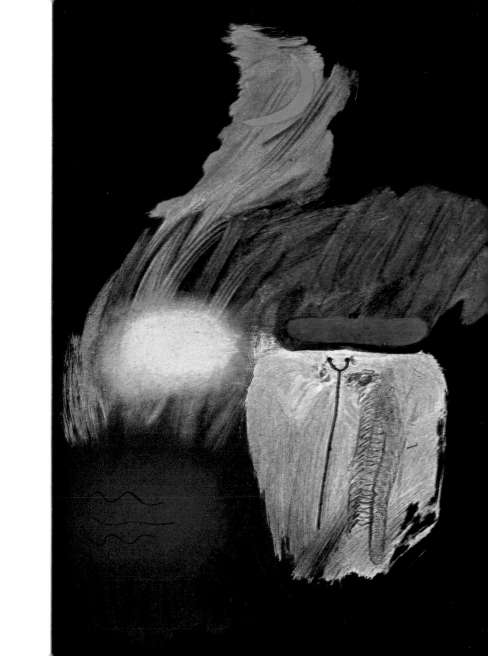

71 Miró: *Head of a Woman*. 1938. Oil. 21⅝ × 18⅛ in. Los Angeles, Private Collection. A monster spawned by the terror of the Spanish Civil War.

72 Miró: *Woman in Front of the Sun*. 1938. Oil. 21⅝ × 18⅛ in. New York, Private Collection. The sun offers warmth and hope to sufferers.

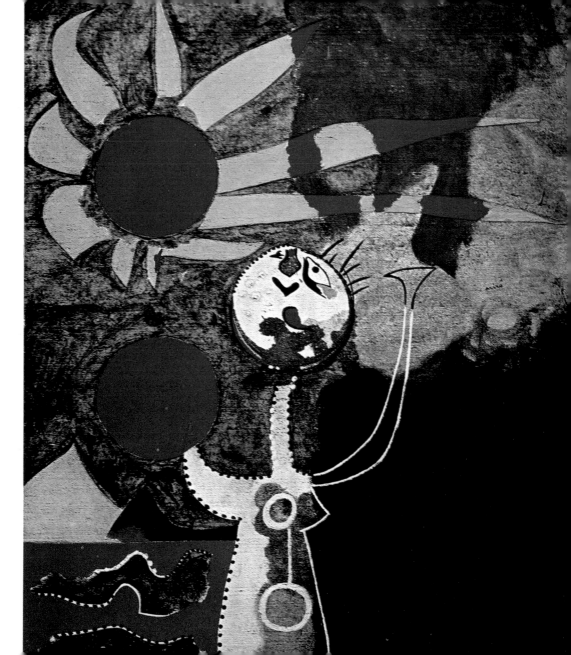

73 Miró: *The Ladder of Escape*. 1938. Oil. 28¾ × 21¼ in, Chicago, Private Collection. By painting on burlap, Miró gives his line added force through contrast.

74 Miró: *Snail, Woman, Flower, Star.* 1934. 76¾ ×67¾ in. Spain, Private Collection. Weird shapes and poetic words intertwine in this composition.

75 Miró: *Personages in the Night Guided by the Phosphorescent Tracks of Snails.* 1940. Oil and gouache. 15 × 18⅛ in. New York, Private Collection. Airy creatures drift across the moon.

76   Miró: *Woman Encircled by the Flight of a Bird*.   1940.   Gouache.   18⅛ × 15 in.   Paris, Private Collection.   Jewels of color are caught in an intricate web.

77 Miró: *Woman and Bird in Front of the Sun.* 1944. Oil. 13¾ × 10⅝ in. Genoa, Private Collection. The symbol-creature appears.

78 Miró: *Painting.* 1944. Oil. Barcelona, Private Collection. An Art Nouveau frame sets off a powerful ideogram.

79 Miró: *Woman and Bird in Front of the Sun*. 1944. Oil. 13¾ × 10⅝ in. Canada, Private Collection. A confrontation under the moon and stars.

80 Miró: *Acrobats in the Night Garden.* 1948. Lithograph. 25½ × 25 in. Colored inks create gay splashes and scrawls.

81 Miró: *Composition*. 1950. Oil. 39 × 29⅞ in. The Netherlands, Eindhoven Art Gallery.
Rope and string echo in three dimensions the ragged shapes of the color blots.

82 Miró: *The Bird Catchers*. 1950. Lithograph. 21⅞ × 15 in. Miró creates a decorative alphabet of his own.

83 Miró: *Series I*. 1952–53. Etching. 15 × 18 in. Creatures of child-like imagining.

84 Miró: *Composition*. 1953. Etching. 9⅞ × 15⅝ in. Disconnected forms somehow express surprise and alarm.

85   Miró: *The Sad Wanderer*.   1955.   Lithograph.   30 × 22 in.   The scrawled accents cohere in a magnificent design.

86 Miró: *The Sun Eater*. 1955. Lithograph. 27⅝ × 21⅝ in. This creature is like a prisoner who sees, and feels, the sun through bars.

87 Miró: *The Sun Wall* (above). 118 × 590 in. *The Moon Wall* (below). 118 × 275 in. 1955–58. Ceramic. Paris, UNESCO Headquarters. Miró's most famous achievement in monumental decoration.

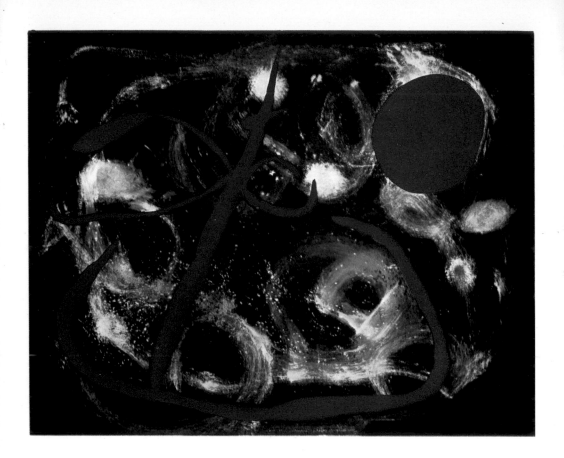

88   Miró: *Joy of a Little Girl in Front of the Sun.*   1960.   Oil.   51⅛ × 63¾ in.   Private Collection.
Another attempt at elemental simplicity of design.

89 Miró: *The Red Disk*. 1960. Oil. **65 × 51** in. New York, Private Collection. A primitive nucleus creates form out of chaos.

90 Miró: *Ceramic* (above). 1955: h. 17¾ in. Paris, Galerie Maeght. *The Face* (below). 1956.
Ceramic. h. 16⅛ in. There is pathos in the attitudes and expressions of these clay creatures.

91 Miró: *Composition*. 1958. Ceramic. Private Collection. There is a suggestion here of an
antique and sacred monument.

92 Miró: *Composition* (above). Ceramic. Private Collection. *Composition* (below). Ceramic. Private Collection. These calligraphic decorations are more carefully controlled.